Fruit Trees

By JOwen

Illustrated by Kara Matters

Library For All Ltd.

Library For All is an Australian not for profit organisation with a mission to make knowledge accessible to all via an innovative digital library solution. Visit us at libraryforall.org

Fruit Trees

First published 2023

Published by Library For All Ltd
Email: info@libraryforall.org
URL: libraryforall.org

Our Yarning logo design by Jason Lee, Bidjipidji Art

Original illustrations by Kara Matters

Fruit Trees
JOwen
ISBN: 978-1-923143-34-0
SKU04307

Fruit Trees

Apple tree

Mango tree

Banana tree

Guava tree

Orange tree

Cherry tree

Pawpaw tree

Plum tree

Lemon tree

Fruit trees give us so much.

You can use these questions to talk about this book with your family, friends and teachers.

What did you learn from this book?

Describe this book in one word. Funny? Scary? Colourful? Interesting?

How did this book make you feel when you finished reading it?

What was your favourite part of this book?

download our reader app
getlibraryforall.org

About the contributors

JOwen is from the Nurrunga/Ngarrindjeri Nations of South Australia. She was born in Adelaide and now lives in Broome, Western Australia. She loves the laughs and fun of family gatherings. As a child, her favourite book was *I Can Jump Puddles*.

Kara is a Noongar artist from Albany, Western Australia, with extensive experience in acrylic painting, digital art, illustration and design. Inspiration comes to Kara in all forms; she draws from the Earth, the Ocean, and what connects her emotionally to Country and soul.

Author's Country

Darwin

NORTHERN
TERRITORY

QUEENSLAND

WESTERN
AUSTRALIA

Perth

SOUTH
AUSTRALIA

Brisbane

NEW SOUTH
WALES

Adelaide

Sydney

ACT
Canberra

Illustrator's Country

VICTORIA
Melbourne

TASMANIA
Hobart

Our Yarning

Want to discover more books from this collection? Our Yarning is a collection of books written by Aboriginal and Torres Strait Islander peoples across Australia.

We know that children learn better, and enjoy reading more, when they see themselves in the stories, characters and illustrations of the books they read.

To download the app, visit the Google Play Store on any Android device and search 'Our Yarning'.

libraryforall.org

www.ingramcontent.com/pod-product-compliance
Lightning Source LLC
Chambersburg PA
CBHW042344040426
42448CB00019B/3399